Table for Three

New and Selected Poems
1982-2021

Lawrence Hopperton

En Route Books & Media, LLC
St. Louis, MO

⊕ENROUTE
Make the time

En Route Books and Media, LLC
5705 Rhodes Avenue
St. Louis, MO 63109

Cover credit: Dr. Sebastian Mahfood, OP

Contact us at
contactus@enroutebooksandmedia.com

LCCN: 2021933681
ISBN-13: 978-1-952464-63-8

Acknowledgments

Some of these poems have appeared in literary magazines including Smeuse (US), Sirsee (US), and Sheila-na-gig (US), and the anthologies Poets 88 (Quarry Press, CAN), Arrivals (The Greenfield Review US), Isms (Lummox Press US) and Tamaracks (Lummox Press US).

A special thanks to Bruce Meyer, Andrew Brooks and James Deahl. We have been on a long, poetic journey together.

Mono Center

Sunshine scents these cliffs, these
leaves pattern the under path.
Insects hum. Springs tangle along
trail away ponds and we are
one last piece finely placed.

Table of Contents

Epigram – Mono Center

Part 1: Spiritus Dei

Part 2: Spiritus Mundi

Spiritus Dei

…I had seen birth and death,
But had thought they were different…

T. S. Eliot, *Journey of the Magi*

Table of records

If it will take the table and benches
with chairs at the ends, I can live there.

Mum and dad brought it home:
mum at this end, dad at that.

Families grow, scrunch together
hogging a favorite dish, or the juice

marks on this come together -
crayon and dog claw, birthday

candle patina sanded, oiled
and finished with knives, forks

a spilled glass. Left-over pot marks
won't wipe away, even scrubbed.

King of the castle

Dreams are real. I am castle king:
cliffs and battlements guard this
parade circling hills and bays.

Someone spoke your name. I turned
and my playground tumbled
around waiting, hoping to see you again.

Book of hours: A ballad

L. Hopperton

Refrain

As you ride by, love
As you ride by,
So I can see you
As you ride by

Roses love sunshine
And violets love dew
The angels in heaven
Know I love you
Refrain

5

Build me a castle
A hundred feet high
So I can see you
As you ride by

Refrain

Each morning at sunrise
I'll climb to the top
To watch for you riding
And wait 'till you stop

Refrain

Each noon I will stand
With the wind in my hair
To watch the green hills
And see you there

Refrain

Each evening at sunset
I'll watch for you, love
And listen for hoof lifts
the moon drift above
Refrain

Each night in the chapel
I'll wait for you, dear
And pray that the angels
Bring you safely here

Refrain

Alone in my bed
I'll be waiting for you
To come and to hold me
Until day is new

Refrain

Your arms are around me
Our hearts beating true
Till then I will wait.
I love only you.

Campfire cards

We light candles outside, enough
for cards we play with bower
bravado, a lanterned forest,
fire steady and low, surrounds
rounds of laughs, a comment,
a lone hand if you are feeling lucky.
Dead wood feeds burning
hot, building embers. It's quiet

like summer at night looks
starring as still air – breathes
weaved words, wiles passing
this moment and candlelight
shadows welcome - eyes glow
like coals. Your skin is smooth.

Twenty-four line loaf

Flour from shelf to table,
powder the bowl measured
by eye. Water and warm:
it is active. Sugar lightly now,
salt and sourdough a week-ago's
ingredients I can never guess.

Your palm-dust rolls.
It presses, covers
with a towel. It rises.
And you spend time with me –
rises and you knead it down again –
rises, and the baking stone

warms the rising to the kitchen,
a pan of water at the bottom,
for the crunchy crust, you say,
because you like it that way.
Baking dishes I never scrub
mushroom over the rims,

It cools on the rack, soon done.
Your arms are around me and
our knife slices the loaf,
steams the flavor of love, golden,
with butter and tomorrow
morning toasted with honey.

Ultrasound

Twelve degrees crystalizes
surfaces all the way down, drains
snowmen to the ground
swells pencil sketched nobs
and branches. Are you alive yet?
The patio recedes under the overhang;
flurries tonight, crocus tips at the edges,
trillium heads, dark green, pine copper.

I saw a chipmunk today, threw nuts
under the spruce skirts relaxing
for the lawnmower. The sun
sets standard time; hawks crest lowly
adjusting air against south walls.
Children laugh down the street
in rain boots resurrected, coat-sleeves
tied at the waist, red cheeks and baby teeth.

Dolphin

Helm hands, calloused, strong
legs straddle the rudder bar.
Steer by compass, feel forward
moods blue and white. Mizzen

main stretch full wind.
A few degrees off, they flop
and everyone knows helm is unsure.
Only landers spin the wheel.

The ship takes time to respond
helm more to compensate.
Trim is the touch. Feel it rush
the deck roll, standard rigging

pulling the sailcloth taut,
the course singing
wheel changes, rudder
angles, how they plow

the sea and you stroke
the canvass ripple rhythms,
surge in winds and ride
the bow waves with the dolphins

Lighting Advent candles

1. The prophecy candle

   Be like daylight today:
   prepare wreaths,
   candles circle our

   come around evergreen
   life, and light
   the world: three blue one pink

   anticipate he comes.
   We know he is coming.
   Oh come Emmanuel.

2. The Bethlehem candle

Waken at the regular
sun and stay in bed like

the children we want to be.
The clock tower birds

chime the morning in and
shadow branches dapple

with strong roots under
cold and clear. Do you hear

the coming? A boy soprano
leads the congregation.

3. The shepherds' candle

Sometime, after a long time
it happens. We rekindle songs

and next week we remember
our promise and we sing

happy swelling anthems
practice more moments with

long voices scratching to go
home, and to come back,

back from schools, the world
comes back. Oh, come raise

voices around the creche
a wreath on our table.

4. The Angels' candle

It's urgent. It come through
evergreens, wakens children.

Story windows and candles
colour the choir and this snow

day carries toboggan voices
fast through branches.

We have hot chocolate
and watch the constellations.

.

Feast of the Nativity

We settle like satin,
coats on shoulder
afternoons, dark nights.
Skies are the depths.
snow falls and tomorrow
on hills children's noses run
like toboggans. Dad brings coffee.

The kitchen starts at noon:
roast beef for 65, potatoes
beets preserved in jars,
rolls and horseradish,
cherry pie, and a floor show:
hymns and poems and harp-songs.
Strike the chorus. Ballads

begin and we sing, we sing
and candles flicker this
midwinter driving home
this silent night almost
ready for stockings.

Birth

Born of wind and wave, mother ship
and the sky, and the water is
beneath the prow - thrusts and sprays
decks swaddled in sailcloth,

lulled by the roll and the rigged hum
all around. Wind and current choose;
the rudder and compass follow.
Your shoulders will scramble up shrouds

from rails to horizon whitecaps,
touch the sky, feel the rocking
heart creak. On the edge of your world
reach the space of sleep.

Cemetery Lane in quarentime

It's just a little fence, only
knee high. I can step over it.
I can lean over it and lift you as high
as our kite flies in my arms,

as fast as breath can pass
stones. Just a few spaces left.
It's busy out there. Roads trail
back to where you came in

and let the children go.
Parks are closed. Mum is bathing.
They come back, well-spaced
families and dogs,

bikes with training-wheels,
scooters with brakes, a toddler
stumbles inside, screaming
what to watch tonight, again.

Kiss this goodnight

I opened the door and said I made
Jimmy Carter's Hawaiian chicken,
confessed I had made up the recipe
with peanuts, and pineapple.

Our sundial evening reaches
filigree fingers, moth wings
where grass has grown rampant
settle. Fold your wings.

'I want to be with you, know you are ok,
our children are safe.' I talk, nothing else. I am
desperate you know love. I love you.
Nothing else is such an only thing really.

They told me hurry the children
to daycare. Come soon,
hold her hand until
time to close her eyes.

Haiku: Lie beautiful

lie beautiful my
       medallion around your neck
again journeys end

An open field

It was an open field.
We flew kites, joked high

density, low-rise sub-divisions.
Vets in one corner, old families,

white crosses and angels in rows,
under the spruce, creeping row on

row, names and dates, numbers
you trip over. Grave diggers

measure, place your stone,
our poem engraved on its back.

Like pneumonia

Time gasps air and shivers stick-feet
in socks, pencils loose in your bed.
Grandchild fingers stroke your hair,
nutcrackers in your sleep, your picture
on a forgotten dock. It sweats
spiced choirs, paraphrased
snowscapes and confidence rates
over cold tea. Can I help with your sweater?

We won't disturb the wreath or candles.
Christ blesses and evergreen branches
twine lights: three blue, one pink
one white. He is coming; He will come.
Oh, come Emmanuel. It's for you, my dear.
Say childhood names, finger
stretch towards turkey and almond
butter in your sleep. Sunrise sweeps

only a moment before it floods –
a moment to rouse and two before
your eyes are closed. Condolent
hymns choke passages, trip the gravesite,
fade to sepia exploring our lonely
pokes, pinched courses and cramps.

Ordinary Sunday

It's early birds and winter windows
I have to clean. Maybe this Sunday
temperatures will rise through
stained glass, dance on the altar.

Robes and lifting song high voices
break this morning. They said your wife died
and I remembered piecelessness.
Use my driveway, my beds I'm home tomorrow.

Your morning starts tired, up anyway
like any day. Go through the routine.
We pray for her, choke hymns, hum
a joyful noise through tears. It's what we do.

Nil nisi bonum

It's raining. No one is surprised.
It was the first snowfall for dad;

January for mum. Guys in rain
gear with shovels over there.

We have umbrellas and prayers
and a little box on a turf-sheet hole

about three and a half feet deep.
It will decay over time.

Everyone said such nice things
and the brothers kept their secrets.

On her death in Australia

Her flicker seeks
flickering. Organs fail
increment by increment.
Her heart is this breath
holding hands. Pumps
manage levels in and out.

I read your letter to her.
She was a bit more there.
I hope she heard it.
Her eyes opened. She said,
"My face hurts and I'm ready
For this game to end.

Vigils are hard

A snow-devil dance
hides my cemetery.
Watch now. Vigils

are hard work: wait
for snowplows to seal
the driveway, emergency

restrictions. You are never ready
when the wait ends. It rained
in Australia. The fire went

The wind blows

Red cheek bedtime
lullaby prayers fight
lights out sleep
now I love you.

Shut down outside
snow and drifting,
the shed the car
closed and dark

breath listens and
bends maple
and ash bone-black
and the wind blows

Punta Cana

Night and diamond eyes dance
on the beach. Your mother was a

wave in and out, toeing the sand
like the samba in your chest

scrapes and scraps
quiet with you is ours.

The children grow along

This deck should be a greenhouse
with depression-glass plates

these grey hairs toasting your
fingers this morning with coffee.

North walls hold this sun trap
under a little melt. The cemetery

piles monumental drifts. Nothing
stops marking how cold it's been.

Auctioneer's song

We will sort the boxes
in the basement, family
furniture no one wants. Accents
are interesting but have no place.

Here are cards and letters
dated childhood in a private place
packed up. Not our memories,
but considered to be sure.

Everything is laid out for viewing
and the auctioneer's song.
Everything else for charity
or the recycling bin.

Morning prayer

Wherever two or more of you

Summer Sunday shines
sweat to the porch doors, to
the narthex greeting friends.
Where is the priest, the process?
Hymns with bits of choir scatter
through the congregation chanting
in old-style; prayer and readings,
a sermon partially scripted

testimonies our chosen
leader chants in thin alto.
We answer the call
and the organ plays us out
side the sanctuary. We linger;
we talk together.

In the beginning

Perspectives reboot. Next,
Leaf buds, shadowing gardens.
Trilliums sprint; annuals root.
crocuses break ground
while it ends. Distance smiles,
wavering just a little. It swirls
outcomes and garden hedge
flowers, yellow, white and red.

Regrets are in the leaves left
under the snow: mouse shelters and bugs.
Fences keep coyotes out. Chipmunks
forage and the earth warms
past the door to the sun deck
with coffee and newspaper.

Lighthouse

an unanticipated need
perhaps the promise to leave
this light to find the way

you have forgotten
the stones gathered one
and one to shore this headland

Ecumenical ice cream

Which one do you want?
Maybe bubble-gum
Or maple walnut?
Me? I'm your butter

pecan escort
to our table - this
seat for you; this one
for me and between

flavors twisting fingers
almost touching tips
perhaps a brush
across our spoons.

Celebration of the word

Come to my place.
It's close and they plow highways first.
I have beds for everyone
red wine, crackers and cheese.

It's a laughing night.
Neighbors stamp the snow
and come in. Doors hold
the snow-devil dancing out.

Snowed in for morning song
but nothing stops. There are shovels;
we have coats and mittens;
plows will come. I sing like at church

with frying pans, omelets and toast
the table for more than two.

Ice storm

Winter screamed high and hard ice
an inch on everything. My grandfathers'
home woke. An oak in a line my father planted
groaned, cracked, fell into silence

maple, pine and birch branches
split down, stripped and tossed, broken
squirrel nests scattered. I will have to
take down the next tree in the line.

It will not stand much longer. My father
heaved the roots, the branches, this story
on my lips, my gloved hands and my chainsaw
rips through, marking me on the line

this place, this time is mine, drying outside-in
and next fall, my son will choose the yule.

Gaudete for baptism

1. Quick

    as your dad can spit fingers across
    your bloody forehead with no crying

    teams of white-coats. Is she alive? Count
    seconds. Counted minutes can be alive.

    Is my wife alive? Call a pastor, somebody
    baptise this counting into a breath if it comes,

    isolate, incubate, save or at least for trying.
    We visit you in intensive care and breast feed

    four days old, breathing when the tower fell.
    Something wrong. Mum needs help.

    Start tests and keep the truth away
    except from me: You know

    we need to talk about termination.
    Yes, but we don't need to talk today.

    This is a permanent condition.
    Yes, but permanent accommodates.

You know your toddler in day care waits.
Yes, but I'll throw up first

then tv and supper time, bedtime stories
and four years later, mum has cancer.

2.   Tower

They closed the ambulance doors
in the middle of the street. Anybody
could see my hands spread, legs
spread. They drive the counting
out: her princess party in palliative care,
Friday flicks on the player our neighbors gave us.

I kissed and you. You kissed back
and were gone. Even the undertaker cried
and I left her to prepare
your mother is dead.
I was with her. She loved
arms around our necks

sink hole empty. Nothing.
No weeping, not yet.

3. Tipple and candle

Baptism Sunday. Mummy and daddy,
baby in arms with God-parents, grandparents,
aunts and uncles and cousins and everyone
crowds and the choir welcomes
our new one and we promise
we will be her congregation.

Was my baptism like that? Did the priest
      hold me?
Did I look at her like I knew something
      was happening?
Did I cry when she poured the water?
Did you snuggle away my fear?

There is only one baptism. Yours
was a moment and God was there.
But we can complete the service if you want.
It was birthright; now it's choice.

Call the children to the altar.
Let them tipple their fingers
in water. Light a candle.
Talk about washing our souls'
promise. The organ plays and choirs
sing your smile into your church.

Prom

Our yard is a canvas you sketched
with light and stretched shadows
filigree topsoil and trilliums.

I try on my strapless bra, my graduation
            dress,
and promise to bring a shawl. You can't
speak; you think I'm beautiful. This

necklace and ring; my shoes
are perfect - your inch of soil, smooth
watering home tonight.

Thanksgiving

settles in cold satin lined
coats on our shoulders; insulated walls
separate the afternoon fading

and skies mirror the bay to its depth.
We harvested frost beets and carrots
to preserve in foundation dirt

with shoulder-high woodpiles. The stove
sparks pine sap. It heats the cabin
corners. Turkey cooks. Dishes clatter,

wash-water warmed in pots.
The atmosphere cools. A radio distorts
draughts across the floor.

Our little one in sleepers with feet
cries, finds mama and hugs a face.
She understands this evening

and tonight there will be stars,
leaves, and gravel roads, rustled marshes,
nine point bucks and branches

migrating rock slopes, red and white pine,
lichen-covered, or needled with leaves,
windswept, and ground slowly carved

knuckle-deep into petroglyphs.
Indian summer doesn't change this.
An outboard motor drones isolate

pine trunks twisting cliffs, acorn hands
clenched in pockets. Our shoulders, our knees
squeeze our bodies small.

A cormorant dances and dives.
It should not be here, not now. Time
kicks at the leaves, at the gravel road.

Pause a moment, our noses running.
Unbuttressed water-coloured
oil-lit tables seat twenty-five,

give thanks for cider and pied
windows, for breath and spider frost
between our resolve and darkness.

Spiritus Mundi

Agnes

1. Perhaps I do

   Misting and shining cobble
   tavern lights to sea, peat
   smoke, something local – Scapa whisky.
   You ask where I'm from. America?
   Africa? All too far away, too foreign

   since you married the neighbor boy
   made children and made them sweaters.
   Now you stop by this pub each evening
   waiting for the boats to come back.
   Between the women laughing

   smoke and drinks we trading tales:
   mine a bit embellished and you
   rolled the sea, rolled the sun
   across the table lashing
   trees you planted, a body

   identified by your sweater.
   Word came. The boats were close
   They would be home soon.
   You stood, said goodbye like tomorrow.
   The bar emptied with you,

a film running down the glass.
But if I had climbed the harbor cliff,
seen your arms locked around your man,
happy the sea had given him backagain,
perhaps I might have a better story.

2. Lament

The sun is low, the wind high and cold
seas surge in strife with the sky.
My body in these days alone
drops to wretchedness.

Since my love was taken by the sea
long as a month is every day
long as a year is every month.
Hours lament. I am an old hag.

Before I lost my love to the sea
sweet was intimacy, sweet the days
my breasts full and firm, lips supple
and my thighs could caress a sailor.

It is not evil that I now wear
a veil of white and grey on my head.
It is evil that I never wore
a wedding veil for my love.
Hours with my love were times of colours:
every hue bedecked my head. My cheek
flushed soft to the touch of his hand,
fields waved golden sunshine to the sea.

Now fire provides me little warmth:
no arm cuddles my shoulder;
no lips welcome me to morning;
no warm breath on my cheek.

My strength has ebbed like the last tide
and I am idle in this harbour.
My cheek has yellowed, my arms are old
bony and thin, an old woman's arms.

Even sleep is no relief for me.
I dream motion to mountains, gushing
waves welling, storms careering and fierce
wind combing white the hair of the sea.

I see sailors awash on stormed decks
losing their grips, their breath in the night.
Their panic swells deeming all is lost
they stretch shipwrecked arms towards the coast.

The wind is high and cold. It pierces
me like a spear. The sea runs high
and the sun rides low in its short course.
My poor body totters, my hands shake.

I have been robbed by the siren sea.
Her song bedevilled my love to death.
I wail to the wind on the water
but these cries never disturb the deep.

Footlocker

It's garbage at the roadside -
We pick it and giggle

treasure into the trunk
disassemble the pieces

strip them and sand the edges
oil-cured, left to dry, sealed

with hand-finished secrets
at the foot of your bed.

Lights in the bush

1. Timberwolf

Darkness creeps into camp and there is no
    moon.
Only occasional words jar the quiet:
shape shadows in brush as broad as the black,
and our eyes reach stars beyond fingertips,
map light with nods focused on this rock
beginning to feel cold through our clothes.
Tonight will not sleep, but our perception
    drowses -
everything as safe as care and luck.

Night turns the constellations, raising mist.
In the moment a tree falls in the dark, tears
    branches,
falling hard and an echo of leaves
settles back. Sense has already tested distance;
will not calm in this silence.
Heartbeats swallow stillness. Only eyes rest.

2. Canyon

> The green-breeze is gone;
> the sun finds south skies.
>
> Insect and bird calls migrate.
> Cloud-tumbles hold scents
> low; snow and rain-drops
> spill black face down.
>
> Ravens ride currents, calls
> echo wall to wall and down.
> A straggler digs a last grub out
> and the land prepares to sleep.
> Little-bloods pile scavenged wood
> on their fire. They huddle close.

3. Chebucto harbor

> You can remember it this way:
> Mist. An undulate call
> ashore; a web of stays
> beat staccato against masts;
> a broad bleached bald rock
> separates constant and fast.

Pitched on its side the sea hollows
rounding pounding plumes
unraveling down dyeing
everything it is not
grudgingly submitting along the line.
Rock-weed roots knot

cracks of random and brine.
Suddenly ankle deep and cold
water, you scramble back to the fine
edge. A shock and rising floods
this isolate fear
this flow of blood. It is still

a harbor relatively staid.
You hear it louder further out.
A black bird, a gull during day
rises over the lapse and wide
water. Eyes dim, blurring
shapes in the falling dark.

At your mark on the line
you no longer see trees or
cottages. They hide. Ozone
breaths stretch-black fingers
to nothing out of reach
shivering trees and spray.

4. Chinook

It skims the lip path, twists the canyon
walls and pines on the rock rim.
Whispers caress your bare arms.
Water swells, ice points peak and blue
snow still on the ground. It whines,

squeezed through the rock fault
And shrikes bounce branch to branch.
Explore this gorge. Listen. There is water.
A cataract flash spill under the crust.
Ice scrapes a vein to bedrock.

You are center. The rapid edge
churning the air swirls rising full
translucent ice and we lean together
back to front, thumbs link through belt
loops, your hair, this flow.

5. Dream time

We are small on the toss. Whales
breach our bit of pontoon, our motor,

fall up back-crash splash another way.
We shiver in our float-suits; try to trust them

and sweat and catch our breath and wait.
Black back spotted spouting, raising tail

flips high and goes straight down.
It won't be back for a few good minutes.

Look! There are two, no three near the cliffs.
One's different-- You can tell by the tail

diving into dream space
off the edges of our rock.

Camp 9

Spiders seek boundaries.
Transitions and tethered
ends triangulate, structure,
grow gossamer forests
with sunscreen and naps.
Swim to the island and back.

Search for wood. Cut the length
and stomp on it. I will teach you to
build tinder and kindling
with games and sawed stories,
and I will rouse you tomorrow
with a morning song; perhaps this one.

Niagara escarpment

Camp Nemo, Halton

Fall was only coming
until the oaks stripped bare.
It rained. Then it stopped.
Then hail winds whipped
our fire high and the dark
dusted frost down this spine
fissured down to snow
that never melts. It's lonely in the cave

and it's cold; November layers up
layers down. We need to rake the yard,
prune the wild rose
scrape the leaves behind the lilac,
and pack in bags out to the curb before
the first snows long melt.

Camp Charl'bro on Big Bay

The escarpment raises its spine and dives
just north of the rain last night driving dark
down ice roads, snow-banks on either side.
They have always told the story here:

Big Bay Ben opens the channels, breaks the ice
with his horn. Spines are pressure points

off White Cloud Island. 40 meters long.
Horns and diamond eyes in the night.
Scouts have seen him. It's recorded:

a photograph they framed in '64
hangs near the hearth in the meeting house
with a stove, outhouses with flashlights

crack the black back. Don't take long.
Morning is coffee. The leaders talk
before they wake the sleeping cabins:

songs for 16 years, saved for this morning.
Twice around walking and slipping;
more footing with snow under the crust.

Pines are birch and overcast backgrounds.
You can almost feel this end time
clear the channels. Evening breaks with wind

thunders visceral thrusts up our legs
ripples not far from this spartan camp.
The ice is broken. Ben is gone.

Camp Daigle

For Marg and Frank

I

It's high water even before spring
culverts flood, the road erodes either
side, ice in the middle, potholes. Snapping

turtles will nest here. Now pressure cracks
the ice like this cold snap. Even sap
stopped running. We collected sixty

liters in plastic jugs these last weeks.
40 to 1 like water from trees.
Boil it down to its secret syrup.

This morning, our eyes closed, tiptoed
past sleeping bags and stoked the wood stove,
chopped wood outside and built a boiling

maple morning day, this afternoon
snow-toffee twist-sticks sample this
time but stay off the lake; stay out of caves.

II

You planned this a year out, didn't tell;
hurried ahead. Made sure it's
back to the birch. Wait for the Dorothy

awe, an emerald cliff, a horse-cart
mine with radiation like a pocket
watch, fissured and fractured.

Gobsmacks and baby fingers explore
the rock face, find samples for geiger
counters and watches from the 40's.

We cower. The icicle mouth snaps
and falls on ducked backs. Call them out
all tired. The syrup boiled all day

down, now 5 degrees above water boiling
at this altitude and morning will have
pancakes with bacon and fried potatoes.

McCraney

What happens at camp stays at camp

1

5:30. Coffee and donuts.
Check the trailer, the canoes,
drive north a half hour late
at the ranger station — they don't care.
Launch at Rain Lake, paddle
the narrows. Stern starboard and
the portage is there. Drag the packs

up the embankment, the canoes.
Load up. It should be fairly easy
kilometers, cart wide, mostly level.
They go to the dam twice a year
through the bush. Walk 10; rest 5.
It's further than you can swat
and then, come back for the rest.

2

It wasn't like that at all. McCraney
with his bum leg canoes for hours.
He doesn't stop deer flies or mosquitoes.
They bite through the narrows, sweating

paddles stroke the lake, swing
south; the portage is that way,
as flat as the forest and wide.
Repellent doesn't work. Wet feet,

arms and legs, socks and hiking shoes
packed tight, with hang-ons, dry-bags,
canoes. Your day pack sweats
in your eyes, bleeding in your shirt —

everything out of slapping reach.
"Ouch! My head! Are we there yet?"

3

One in front. Keep moving.
Rest. Keep moving. Rest.
Your water bottle. Load and
launch ahead but nobody said

leeches or this beaver dam.
"McCraney, it's one of your poems!"
Step delicate, slide down easy:
lily-pads, underwater dead

heads and frogs all the way.
This lake has no reeds
no shallows only driftwood shores.
The dam is closed. The fish are deep.

Camp on the east side of the island
sheltered with rods and painted lures
past the cliff with anchoring roots.
Beach, steady. Unload. Steady.

4

You will see stars from here,
fledgling loons, thunder moon,
sunrise trees, the lake laugh,
shoulders glister like muscle

memory flying forward as fast
as a blue canoe can go
past the island all the way.
Bushwhack barefoot if you have to.

We're this close, this back-water bower
painted green with rusty chains, holds
spill-down four meters high. Nothing
too far; white water in town.

Paddle the Don:
Toronto Conservation Authority

Come in bow first at weir one.
They will catch you, swing your stern
around and lift you out, ready
for 300 more. Portage. Paddle.
Weir two is easy coming in. The artery
calms. If you haven't dumped yet
you probably won't. The portage is level
and we are stationed to launch your next leg.

Another canoe slides down another
easy water to our knees. Adolescents
watch the river, rank distractions
and laugh, launch the rapids. You can run them
if you want to. We're behind you just in case.
Then the safety sweep comes through.

Hemlock
after David Wevill

My chair is an afternoon sundial, watching
the movement of poems and young boys
talking about cars and tits, bragging about farts.
I want this spending a warm afternoon.

Our fire burns to cooking coals. Find water.
Boil it. You can't be sure anymore.
Dinner is almost ready. Get your mess kits
this mosquito afternoon. Sprays and lotions,

cover-ups almost work. Don't scratch –
itches just get bigger. Let your beards grow
out for your new land. They will hide
pimples and we will billow

atlantic cliffs – white and full like mine
or scruffy, new and mostly blond. I cut mine
back and back again to hide the truth:
You are ready to go alone.

'We want you to come because it's fun.
You have stories we want to hear.
         But sometimes
we don't understand your jokes and you
don't care about wireless reception.'

War canoe

stroke
one broad back

stroke
leave the man down

stroke
he won't drown

stroke
oh the year was 1778

stroke
how I wish I was in Sherbrooke now

stroke
stop port

stroke
starboard cut

stroke
to the stern

stroke
breathes our blue canoe

stroke
and finish for the cameras

Trinity Bay

Tree lines, as high as foghorns
boom the combers, echoing

ice bergs. Plovers fly;
puffins on the bob can't.

Their bellies are too full. The tide
carries away this wharf, this

edge of earth. Except for tourists,
the town is almost as empty

as ice storms pressing tombstones
over. Your history remembers

stories climbing cliffs, the sea call.
The post office hopes for letters

that almost never come, but you
will come back and mumble,

"See you dad. Paul's in from God's
cove; been working the mussels."

Palgrave

This cabin in the hills was payment for service
in the war of 1812. Cedar beams two-feet
wide all the way up are walls with mortar
rippled windows, red squirrels in the roof

chipmunks on tables when we unlock the door.
What's left is a few boxes. The junk man
Tuesday; the sale closes Wednesday
and it's going to be knocked down.

My grandparents are buried just over there.
You can see the corner of the cemetery.
We sprinkled my parents' ashes there
And played baseball in the low area.

Draw a line from the hill to the crossroad
back and follow the fence. That's square here.
It was bigger before but how much farmland
does a soldier and horse really need?

He shaped the wood for a long time.
Dove-tailed the delicate bits
pegs in the perfect spot to seal the roof
for at least the next few generations.

The nearest flowing water is the
        Nottawasaga,
a few miles north-west from here.
There is a well, but I wouldn't drink it
        now
not with all the chemical farming

Finch

Maple and elm border
snow: some time, now, its winter.

Glass heat vents, and outside
maple, elm, and dogwood

sticks. It's hard to tell. Pine and
white sky feed a storm frenzy

slow. Tomorrow morning
at the back door, watching

you drag a wing as cats roam,
as feeding eyes dart almost

round, intent distracting:
where is my mate?

Olive shoulders, yellow
bib breasted goldfinch white:

white rump, a black tail dandy
weed, and vine and catkin strain

esophagus full fledged
where is my mate?

brown-black shoulders
dart gold, olive and glass.

Ordinary time

Pail winter out of the gutters
down the ladder. Clean the yard:
shift rocks, dig gardens, cautious
petals, tentative steps. Seeds germinate.
Cedar and wild rose, clematis and maples
trimmed tall flower. Tulips draw
       groundwater
and the grass is short for the first time;
a ruddy mower; a wheelbarrow
and topsoil on patio stones.
forget roots and fingernail dirt.
Children squeal on the road out front
garbage and recycle on Thursday.

Getting ready

Lay lime in shade spots;
neutralize the soil for what might
grow in an exploding fade.
The lawnmower won't start.
Fill it. Check the oil and prime it.
Pull the cord, prime it check
the oil and pull. Well done.
We need seed and topsoil. We should

think about growing under the maples,
We can plant hostas. They grow in
rough spots. Tonight should rain;
tomorrow topsoil when the sun warms.
A cardinal on the fence scans for his mate,
watches for rain. We'll see if it works.

Dog days

Hot, and heavy like rain
spots on the deck.
We wish there was more.
My shirt sticks. The dog
lounges in the wading pool.
Her friend looks for space
on this dog day reaching out
without breath, waiting
for the sun to fade
but the heat doesn't.

We air condition – 5 degrees
below outside – and we sweat.
The cat drowses in shadows
her belly up; too hot to play.
The mower in the garage rusts
like the lawn. Wildflowers seed
this dormant time. Pray for rain
and it will grow. If not, the water bill
is the cost of inheriting
but at least there is water.

Seat of Wisdom in Barry's Bay

You wonder when you drive into the bush:
are the roads marked; do they match the map?
What about washouts or roads with detours
only locals know. A few cottages string the lake

stretch forests over hills like a green
blanket with a town - a hamlet really - on the way
somewhere no one goes with dirt roads
and a steeple everyone can see.

Downtown is six stores at the crossroad
a restaurant and beer store down
where the trees start, closed on Tuesdays.
But cars stop if you want to cross the road.

A fishing boat speaks polish, drifts
as still as dog-day afternoons.
Our Lady needs help with the pandemic:
they promised first year online and have

nothing in place except this outsider
in a mask with a month before launch.
Air ripples west to east and tonight
will be silent-dark as all the stars.

The moon wanes over my cottage
a short walk to school, but everything is.
Deer steal past: two does and a young buck
on watch to sound the alarm if I move.

He waits. The does forage and fade
into the bush. He follows into too dark
to see; mosquitoes are free and morning
brings a covid challenge and no coffee.

Martello Tower

It sweated Princess Street to the lake
squatted on Wolfe Island
reflected off the Kingston limestone.
It idled the afternoon –
peeled clothes, burned shoulders, stalled
into evening blanketing tonight.

On dormitory steps every light
feels hot. Headlights creep for a slow
breeze, round the corner, reflect
the haze on bushes, bare legs,
the Martello tower.
We become mysterious

responses, separated seeking
our element in the lake,
drop our clothes behind the concession.
Our hot skins finely stripped
approach surrender and wade
into welcome between our pores

and water combining shapes,
textures, temperatures in
concurrent centered circles,
cools our bodies into a drifting
past the harbor lights, the breakwater
between islands to the St. Lawrence.

Tipple fingers

Fishing boats come home.
across the rippled light adrift
and taut as canvas and rope.

This pleasure scents our skin,
your bronze texture, step stones
and pinecones, bare shoulders

sun and beach lap your toes first,
inch up your ankles, your knees,
creeping to your core

your arms stretched out
your fingers anticipate arching
water. Stroke the channel.

Ptolley Bay

"…her eyes are far already."
Stephen Spender, *To my daughter*

Cottage shadows define south and the time of day.
There are deer tracks down the path in. You see
    them
past the gardens you created between the rocks.
Your stone skips seven times. A daring
    chipmunk
with a bald spot demands another peanut.
You hold one out, tap the deck, and it takes it
slowly, tugging your thumb and finger. You
caress its belly. It runs but comes back.

You swim to the island and back –Olympic
pools, maybe three and deep. The bay is like that
one way, ninety seconds, hugging shoulders
"I did it, didn't I dad?" Your hair, your arm
we grin something, paddle home
dipping Polaris, our glass lake lullabye.

Anchor the dock

We will use the 6 x 6 to measure
the distance for the holes in the bedrock
and drill down, and set anchor bars for the dock
and the boats and the water level this year.
Last summer was lower. The dock just floated.

Last winter ice was as thick as the snowpack
and it all melted. It unhinged docks and they
    floated away.
It's 14 inches higher than last July, but that was low.
We need options; holes in the granite drilled to
    powder.
Set rebar anchors just in case the water is higher.

We pay flat rate for the drill, not the holes.
Pour the lake down. Cool the bit,
Flush the dust out or it binds your hands,
spins back the cord around your legs.
A bit of blood; a bit of water back to work.

A hole to let ice split the rock.
We teach you to try to shape landscapes --
water rises or falls and we come back each year
rent the drill and the generator.
The holes drop to ten dollars each.

Fire season

Swimming summer expects
perhaps an eye: kids
swamp a canoe, laugh
at cell-phone videos.

There are pictures of this place from before
the burnt-out logs over there
were an ice-house; a wharf squared those
two points, tethered fishing moorings.

The cabin on the cliff is my usual place.
Tree tops sleep and breathes soundings
off the lake. Leaves brush the dark
drips. Maybe more. Thunder

counts by thousands. It's far from
our dry watch lightning started
in '58. It would be sad to see it go
what with high water.

This year, a book, a beer and
kids paddle into the bay.
You feel it in your throat first –
channel smoke from 20 miles north.

Fire boats siren up the channel.
How far away are we? You listen
to the radio. We will get out if it comes;
scrape together comeback if we have to.

Greenman

Trees with widow-makers shadow
the deck-top, the path to the bush.
You weed beans, plant annuals, perennial
paths in pots from the deck to the dock,
keep the buildings up. Always something to do –

change the water flow under the foundation,
insulate for two more months.
No one comes in February.
They don't come at night either.
Roads run. Deer eyes reflect

and you might stop. Moose eyes don't.
They happen like record high
water. You moved the docks up
and there is no beach anymore.
My son helped drill anchor holes

for low water, your space,
this family place in treetops.
The earth will take you for forest
walks after coffee, soil found in gullies
brought back to bury plumbing

environmentally neutral, except
the wood stove in winter.
Spring stars tend ice holes,
a canoe for your love and leaves
in your hair. You set bugs free.

Brulé Lake

Last spring, the melt water in Rosswood
rose over its old beaver dam
and started trickling, taking first
leaves still decaying from last fall,
then decay from the fall before,
mud and stronger branches and logs
chewed to size and slapped into place.
It burst. Below Brule turned black
and all the trout died in the silt.

You canoed this route a year ago,
carved a campsite in the bush
and drank its clear water;
canoed again this year, found
low water, two dead lakes. Across
Brule you dig and fill sandbags,
paddle them back, sweat a thousand
paces through the bush, and lay them
where what's left of the dam still stands.

Months from now, the first leaves will fall;
will be months before the last snow falls;
melt water run-off fills the lakes.
And you may portage this way again
drop a fishing hook and anticipate trout.

Isle of Barra

It's a little rounding out
waves and batten skies,
moor-green and grey mist
in crash and day spray.
Hair wind-tangle drips
down my neck, in my eyes,
flowers and grass to my knees,
my feet ankle deep. Only

one little road to the jetty built
as high as the sea can over-reach
on high days. No trees. Few
cars, fewer houses, only
sheep dot far and white, and pack
straps strain my shoulders together
heavy on hips and knees.
A dog hidden on the moor barked –

a sentry with wide eyes
in the grass: matted fur, white
muzzle and legs and pained walk.
Her growl didn't frighten:
teats swung, she waddled
slow, sniffed, wagging just
the tip, tail, whole body
head turned to a scratched ear.

I rub her haunches; run my hands
over her ribs. She nudges her snout
to my nose, licks my ear and I trust
my hand in her mouth.
The sea spray split pitches
high over my ferry prow;
My girl watches from the jetty
fading into going on.

Ultima thule

rises tree-tip high and stands by itself in the
    sea,
with leaves. Wildwoods touch autumn
born in sun, bathed in mountain streams,

play towers near the surf. Fists full of sand
and thin footprints lead stretch-tide
blown blaze-running horizons.

Iona

Beyond the sound this island greens
rainbows, sea-blue, heather
purple and thistles burst their bulbs
beating wings, terns and gulls.

Children in short pants run through
centuries. Saints sleep. Rising suns
wave wind and the world
beats slow, drifting in light.

Epigraph

Benediction

Joy giver, you give us,
all of us, all we need
food and water for thirst.

Air snaps our noses in morning
light measures our evening west
and we thank you this night

in this space we care for
like the children we are
children wanting to be.